Quotes to Nirvana

John Taylor Wood

May 1, 2010
www.philosophizeinc.com

A Philosophize Inc. Production
iUniverse, Inc.
New York Bloomington

Quotes to Nirvana

iUniverse books may be ordered through booksellers or by contacting:

iUniverse
1663 Liberty Drive
Bloomington, IN 47403
www.iuniverse.com
1-800-Authors (1-800-288-4677)

ISBN: 978-1-4502-1042-3 (pbk)
ISBN: 978-1-4502-1041-6 (ebk)

Printed in the United States of America
iUniverse rev. date: 11/5/2010

INTRODUCTION

NIRVANA GOAL

Translations of Buddha's work help us learn about truth, love and Nirvana. The goal of every human should be to reach the highest level possible, the state of Nirvana, using their God given ability. Nirvana is a passionless peace within oneself; freedom from pain, worry and the external world. When one reaches Nirvana, as did Buddha, insight and knowledge are realized. In other words Nirvana is a state of wisdom, happiness, contentment, lack of material desire and the sense of doing God's will. Death is of no concern.

An eight-fold path, as described by Buddha, leads to Nirvana. All folds must be taken simultaneously to reach the goal. The folds are: effort, conduct, mindfulness, concentration, purpose, understanding, speech and vocation.

Quotes to Nirvana, is composed of famous quotes from some of the best minds in world history. These words of wisdom are categorized using the eight-fold path of Buddha. Sub categories of each fold provide a more vivid definition. The aim of this book is to help mankind, through quotes, to understand how to reach Nirvana. I wish you good reading, good changing, good luck and good living.

John Taylor Wood October 7, 2009

"Take the understanding of the East and the knowledge of the West- and then seek."

Gurdjieff

L-R: Jim Martin, Illustrator; James Clifton, Creative Consultant; John Taylor Wood, Author

The One Library located at The Gallery, 230 West 3rd, Davenport, Iowa, 52804

Procurator, James

CREDITS

Why God gave me so little ability and a goal to improve mankind has got to be one of the funniest acts to follow in Heaven. Everything about me is just mediocre. Yet, at age 65, I am living proof a good person can be average. Aristotle produced the Doctrine of the Mean which says the ideal is in the middle, avoid the extremes. I wrote this quote: "It takes a good person to know a good person; unfortunately few know me."

I did not actually write this book, Quotes To Nirvana. I am the organizer. The Lord showed me the way to work with others, solicit help from others and keep an open mind. He taught me to be as honest as is humanly possible. The great Mohammad received one motivating word from God, "RECITE!" My directional word was, "TYPE!" Mohammad had no scholarly training, no command of Arabic writing. He wondered how he could communicate the word of God, but it happened. Now me; I never took a typing lesson. I received a computer for my vocation, and as a salesman selling my tools to industry, I had to master the basic essentials. In retirement as I work my hobby of collecting quotes from great minds, I am baffled at how quickly all my fingers move to "TYPE" a new quote for my file. All of my typing, with the Lord's assistance, has produced this book, Quotes to Nirvana. I believe God touched the lives of each and every person who made a quote that guides humanity toward Heaven. Therefore this book pools together the work of God with people throughout the history of mankind.

THANKS

First and foremost I thank God. I thank him for my existence even though certain elements of a basic human were left out of my formulation. Several of my former customers told me that God broke the mold from which I was made. One is enough. Having spent decades of my working life in foundries and watching millions of castings being produced, I understand the loss of producing a defective mold. Some castings, like humans from Heaven, need to be cleaned with abrasive products like grinding wheels and sandpaper that rid a shape of undesirable material. The quotes in Quotes to Nirvana will grind away at human defects. This is best understood by this quote from Jacob M. Braude, "Life is a grindstone, whether it grinds you down or polishes you up depends on what you're made of."

I need to pay tribute to Benjamin Franklin who popularized quotes in his Poor Richard's Almanac versions. His genius has profound influence on mankind. Many of his quotes are heard all the time. Also, he planned the first library. My hangout while in college was the Enoch Pratt Free Library in Baltimore, Maryland. My research projects were made possible by this institution.

Next, I wish to thank my beloved mother, Elizabeth Channel Wood, who encouraged me through my formal education. This Goucher College graduate, teacher, Girl Scout leader, church leader and mother was a hard working, brilliant person.

James Clifton of Davenport, Iowa used his religious knowledge to guide my organization of quotes by Buddha's eight paths. I could not have done this book without James. Our many meetings in the Coffee Dive of downtown Davenport were always informative, funny and productive. James also received a one word commandment from

God, "INSIGHT." He used his abilities to guide me in categorizing, indexing and editing all the quotes under consideration. James is a Creative Consultant of Philosophize Inc.

Jim Martin of Davenport, Iowa, is the Illustrator for the book. He has been drawing cartoons since grade school. He has had many great art teachers in the past. During two years of study at Saint Ambrose University in Davenport, he took many of their art courses. With James and I running ideas through his head faster than his pencil could move, he always returned with a beautiful compromise. Jim is an important part of Philosophize, Inc.

My wife, Nancy, helped me immensely. While she worked a stressful full time job, she always was ready to edit my work. Oh how she loves to show me better wording, grammar and punctuation. Without it, I would be a worthless ego maniac.

My former employer and his wife, Don and Charlotte Williams, were gracious capitalists. They ran a company, Don E. Williams Co. (DEWCO) using most of the principles in this book. Their management not only provided me and my family with adequate income, medical insurance and college scholarships, but an ESOP (Employee Stock Owned Plan) that resulted in a comfortable retirement, allowing me time to write this book.

Randy Emerson, a computer genius and former V-P over the IT Dept. of DEWCO, created my web pages. His work is very important to the book, Philosophize Inc. and our customers.

Finally, I want to thank the employees of my company, Philosophize Inc. Their work of editing and suggesting new ideas was invaluable to me. We work, and have fun doing it. With motivation from above, we can assist other people in living better lives. We don't have a building as yet, so I am indebted to many of the coffee shops located in the Quad-Cities for providing us space to work on this book, particularly the Coffee Dive on 3rd St. in Davenport. You may look forward to many more pieces of art produced by Philosophize Inc.

How To Use This Book –

QUOTES TO NIRVANA

1. Memorize your favorites for instant recital at any time.

2. Leave a quote note for others to find and ponder. Could be a wakeup call or appreciation for a good deed.

3. Redirect your life using the quotes that attack your faults.

4. Use your favorite quotes to build self confidence.

5. Study the authors of your favorite quotes.

6. Have group discussions with your friends and acquaintances.

7. Get your favorite quotes printed and preserved in a first class fashion.

Philosophize Inc. can get it printed, engraved or embossed on paper, wood, metal, rock, glass, plastic or cloth. See the ad on page 63.

8. Design an educational program to study the merits of these quotes at church, school, business, parties, etc.

9. Send a quote for book II. If it is used, Philosophize Inc. will reward you. I also welcome your comments and suggestions.

Keep it short, simple and universal. See the ad on page 63.

10. Play a game: guess the author, guess the category, guess the path. Read a quote. Then guess whether it is exact or altered. Pick a topic, then read the quotes and relate them to your life.

The Eight-Fold Path of Shakya Muni (Buddha)

1. EFFORT – energy you apply; exertion of power, physical or mental; something done by exertion

2. CONDUCT – how a person acts, behavior

3. MINDFULNESS – present in the moment – now, consciousness

4. CONCENTRATION – attentive, careful, focus

5. PURPOSE - of a person – true to yourself; the object for which anything exists or is done, made, used; motive; an intended or desired result, end aim.

6. UNDERSTANDING – knowledge – to perceive the meaning of, grasp the idea of, comprehend insight, perception

7. SPEECH – vocabulary, context, communicate

8. VOCATION – duty - job

   Clergy/Scholar/Teacher

   Administrator/Military

   Merchant/Farmer/Entertainer

   Laborer/Public Servant

CONTENTS

EFFORT

When you find yourself in a hole,
quit digging.

EFFORT

ACTION

Don't wait for the ship to come in. Row out and meet it.

If you put a crow in a cage, will it talk like a parrot?

All human actions have one of these causes: chance, nature, compulsion, habit, reason, passion and desire.

ABILITY

The superior man is distressed by his want of ability. Confucius

ATTRACTION

A little bait catches a large fish.

CURE

Are you going to cure or ignore? John Taylor Wood

DETERMINATION

Fall seven times, stand up the eighth time.

DOING

When you can do the common things of life in an uncommon way, you'll command the attention of the world. Jimmy Carter

You keep on getting what you're getting when you keep on doing what you've been doing.

Do it! Move it! Make it happen! No one ever sat their way to success.

Do what you can, with what you have, where you are. Theodore Roosevelt

What we have to learn, we learn by doing. Aris

Well done is better than well said. Benjamin Franklin

Act in such a rational way that what you do could become a universal law. Immanuel Kant

What you do not want done to yourself, do not do to others. Confucius

We are what we repeatedly do. Aristotle

Don't let what you can not do interfere with what you can do.

There is never a wrong time to do the right thing.

All the things I really like to do are either immoral, illegal or fattening. Woollcott

Always do right. This will gratify some people, and astonish the rest. Mark Twain

EXERCISE

Anyone whose thoughts are much absorbed in some intellectual pursuits must allow his body to efface due exercise and practice gymnastics. Plato

Don't go to the gym for the hell of it. Go for the health of it. John Taylor Wood

HABIT

Who is strong? He that can conquer his bad habits. Benjamin Franklin

I never knew a person to overcome a bad habit gradually.

Men's natures are alike; it is their habits that carry them far apart. Confucius

To cease smoking is the easiest thing I ever did. I ought to know because I've done it a thousand times. Mark Twain

HOSPITALITY

Food without hospitality is a medicine.

INACTIVE

A man will rust out sooner than he will wear out. Colonel Sanders of KFC

By sleeping we do not gain money; by sitting no fortune be had.

LITTLE

From a spark of fire, a heap of coals is kindled.

A spoon full of tar in a barrel of honey and all is ruined.

The needle is small, but pierces sharply.

Don't despise pepper because it is so small; eat, and see how pungent it is.

NEARNESS

Being close only counts in three activities: horseshoes, hand grenades and ballroom dancing.

PAIN

No honey without a sting; no rose without a thorn.

PRACTICE

Practice what you preach.

Practice makes perfect.

QUITTING

Being defeated is often only a temporary condition. Giving up is what makes it permanent.

The man that wins may have been counted out several times, but he didn't hear the referee.

Never, never, never give up.

RESPONSIBILITY

To see what is right, and not do it is want of courage, or of principle. Confucius

REWARD

A lean award is better than a fat judgment. Benjamin Franklin

He that will eat the kernel must crack the nut.

SELF-RELIANCE

Self-reliance is like a flashlight; no matter how dark it gets, it will help you find your way.

SPORTS

Champions never complain. They're busy getting better.

STRAIN

The cord of a violin is broken in stretching it too much.

A diamond is a chunk of coal made good under pressure.

UNITY

Two heads are better than one.

We must indeed all hang together, or most assuredly, we shall all hang separately. Benjamin Franklin

If you can't beat'em, join,em.

Birds of a feather flock together.

Talent may win games, but teamwork and intelligence wins championships.

Food served in the house of a united family is enjoyable.

Trees which stand in a clump, resist the fiercest winds, owing to their mutual support. Mahabharat

WORK

Keep your nose to the grindstone.

Success comes before work only in the dictionary.

When you find yourself in a hole, quit digging.

When the field was sown without being plowed, it yielded without being reaped.

The energy spent on active inner work is then and there transformed into fresh supply, but that spent on passive work is lost forever. Gurdjieff

If you don't want to work, you have to work to earn enough money so that you won't have to work. Ogden Nash

The harder you work, the luckier you get.

GENERAL

Nothing prospers without effort. Sophocles

What can't be done easily rarely gets done. John Taylor Wood

When you can't change the direction of the wind, adjust your sails.

The greater the price in effort, the greater the reward.

CONDUCT

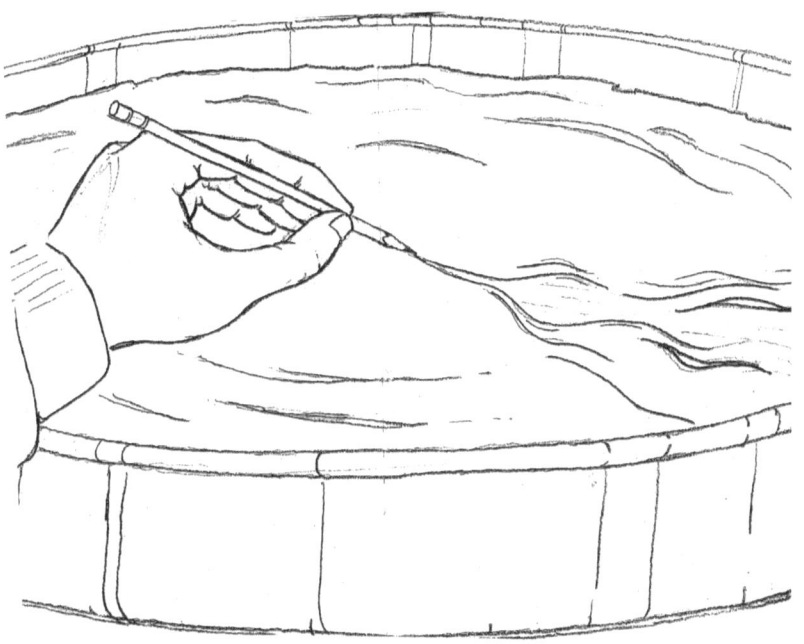

Worldly prosperity is like writing on water.

CONDUCT

ANGER

Anger warms the invention, but overheats the oven. Benjamin Franklin

When angry, count four; when very angry, swear. Mark Twain

Anger does great damage to the vessel it is stored in as it does to anything it is poured upon.

Science is the remedy for anger.

Whoever restrains himself his anger when he has the power to show it, God will give him a great reward.

Power consists in not being able to strike another, but in being able to control oneself when anger arises.

The superior man is satisfied and composed; the mean man is always full of distress. Confucius

Anger is the fire of the heart.

When you have to kill a man it costs nothing to be polite. Winston Churchill

From morning until night and from night until morning keep your heart free from malice towards anyone.

It is hard to be angry in the presence of imperturbable good-nature. It is well-nigh impossible to be morose in the face of cheerful and generous helpfulness.

Anger has no eyes.

Aggression unopposed becomes a dangerous disease. Jimmy Carter

CANDOR

Straightforwardness, without the rules of propriety, becomes rudeness. Confucius

CHARITY

Proportion your charity to the strength of your estate, or God will proportion your estate to the weakness of your charity. Benjamin Franklin

DECEIVED

Who has deceived thee so oft as thy self? Benjamin Franklin

DESIRE

Let thy discontents be secret. Benjamin Franklin

Who has reached the limit of desire?

DISCONTENTED

The discontented man finds no easy chair. Benjamin Franklin

DISCRETION

You may give a man an office, but you cannot give him discretion. Benjamin Franklin

DISHONEST

Prefer a loss to a dishonest gain; the one brings pain at the moment, the other all the time.

DRINKING

When the wine enters, out goes the truth.

I have gotten more out of smoking and drinking than smoking and drinking got out of me. Winston Churchill

EAT

Eat to live, and not live to eat. Benjamin Franklin

Three good meals a day is bad living. Benjamin Franklin

To lengthen the life, lessen the meals. Benjamin Franklin

What one relishes, nourishes. Benjamin Franklin

No wonder Tom grows fat, the unwieldy sinner makes his whole life but one continual dinner. Benjamin Franklin

Eat to please thyself, but dress to please others. Benjamin Franklin

Eat not to dullness; drink not to elevation. Benjamin Franklin

ENVY

Envy is a raging fever; envy has no rest; the wise no poverty.

Keep yourself from envy, because it eats up and takes away good actions as fire consumes and burns wood.

EXCELLENCE

The quality of a person's life is in direct proportion to their commitment to excellence, regardless of their chosen fields of endeavor.

Excellence is never an accident.

FAMILIARITY

Familiarity breeds contempt … and children. Mark Twain

FOOL

Only a fool falls twice in the same hole.

FORGIVE

Forgive and forget. Sour grapes make for lousy wine.

GENEROSITY

Real generosity is doing something nice for someone who'll never find out.

GIFTS

Never spare the parson's wine, nor barers pudding. Benjamin Franklin

Give in this world. Receive in the next.

You may not carry away with you but those things which you have given.

GLUTTONY

The excess of joy is sorrow; of wine drunkenness.

More export than import to prevent a portly pot. John Taylor Wood

What you eat in private is for the world to see.

TOPS

No food tastes as good as thin feels. Weight Watchers

I eat to live, and also, it so happens to enjoy, but I do not eat for the sake of enjoyment. Mahatma Gandhi

GREED

Poverty wants some things, luxury many things, avarice all things. Benjamin Franklin

The white man knows how to make anything, but he does not know how to distribute it. Sitting Bull

A fool and his money are soon parted.

What is a man if he is not a thief who openly charges as much as he can for the goods he sells? Mahatma Gandhi

GREETING

Good greeting softens the cat.

HUMILITY

To be humble to superiors is duty, to equals courteous, to inferiors nobleness. Benjamin Franklin

No one can make you feel inferior without your consent. Eleanor Roosevelt

Honesty is the first chapter in the book of wisdom.

Greet those whom you know and those whom you don't know.

INSULTS

Backbiting is more grievious than adultery, and God will not forgive the backbiter until the one wronged has forgiven him.

JUDGMENT

When you judge others, you are revealing your own fears and prejudices.

Let the refining and improving of your own life keep you so busy that you have little time to consider others.

Don't judge a man by the tales of others. Gurdjieff

What the superior man seeks is in himself. What the mean man seeks is in others. Confucius

KINDNESS

Kindness is the kind of language the deaf can hear and the dumb can understand.

Always be a little kinder than necessary.

You cannot do a kindness too soon, for you never know how soon it will be too late. Ralph Waldo Emerson

A dog instinctively recognizes the kindness shown to it; how base is man who feels not the good that is done to him.

LEND

Lend money to an enemy, and thou'lt gain him, to a friend and thou'lt lose him. Benjamin Franklin

LYING

Lying rides upon debt's back. Benjamin Franklin

There are three kinds of lies: lies, damn lies and statistics. Mark Twain

What a tangled web we weave when first practice to deceive.

MODESTY

Great modesty often hides great merit. Benjamin Franklin

Tho modesty is a virtue, bashfulness is a vice. Benjamin Franklin

MORALS

Morals are an acquirement- like music, like a foreign language, like piety, poker, paralysis- no man is born with them. Mark Twain

PARDON

It is surely better to pardon too much than to condemn too much.

PITY

Great souls with gen'rous pity melt; which coward tyrants never felt. Benjamin Franklin

PRAISE

Praise little, dispraise less. Benjamin Franklin

PRIDE

The blind can not see. The proud will not.

No greater enemy than pride.

Good breeding consists in concealing how much we think of ourselves and how little we think of the other person. Mark Twain

When you meet someone better than yourself, turn your thoughts to becoming his equal.

No standing in the world without stooping.

When you meet someone not as good as you are, look within and examine your own self. Confucius

Pride is as a good a beggar as want, and a great deal more saucy. Benjamin Franklin

Vain-glory flourish, but beareth no fruit. Benjamin Franklin

PRINCIPLES

In the matters of style, swim with the current; in matters of principle, stand like a rock.

PROSPERITY

Prosperity discovers vice, adversity virtue. Benjamin Franklin

QUALITY

Desire to have things done quickly prevents their being done thoroughly. Confucius

Let your policy be quality.

There is always time to do it twice, but never time to do it right.

SECRET

Three may keep a secret if two of them are dead. Benjamin Franklin

SELFISH

No one is disgusted with his own bad smell.

SIN

Though a man may remove the distance of fifty miles, his sin is still with him.

The contemplation of vice is a vice.

She commits the sin and blames Satan for it.

SLOTH

Treat everyone as you would like to be treated yourself.

Never leave that till tomorrow which you can do today. Benjamin Franklin

STEAL

Look not at the thieves eating meat, but look at them suffering punishment.

STUPIDITY

When I was a boy of 14 my father was so ignorant I could hardly stand to have the old man around. But when I got to be 21, I was astonished at how much he had learned in 7 years. Mark Twain

Never approach a bull from the front, a horse from the rear, or a fool from any direction. Danny Saradon

Nothing in the world is more dangerous than sincere ignorance and conscientious stupidity. Martin Luther King Jr.

SUICIDE

Nine men in ten are suicides. Benjamin Franklin

SURRENDER

A part of the excellence of a man's surrender is his leaving alone what does not concern him. Mohammad

TEMPTATIONS

There are several good protections against temptations, but the surest is cowardice. Mark Twain

TRUST

Trust thy self, and another shall not betray thee. Benjamin Franklin

TYRANT

The big fish lives on little ones.

VICE

What maintains one vice would bring up two children. Benjamin Franklin

The second vice is lying; the first is running into debt.

Let thy vices die before thee. Benjamin Franklin

WEALTH

Who is rich? He that rejoices in his portion. Benjamin Franklin

He does not posses wealth, it posseses him. Benjamin Franklin

Wealth is not his that has it, but his that enjoys it. Benjamin Franklin

Worldly prosperity is like writing on water.

In a country well governed poverty is something to be ashamed of. In a country badly governed wealth is something to be ashamed of. Confucius

If you'd know the value of money, go borrow some. Benjamin Franklin

Pay what you owe, and what your worth you'll know. Benjamin Franklin

Nothing but money is sweeter than honey. Benjamin Franklin

When the good man gets riches, it is like fruit falling in the midst of a village.

Wealth is but manure, useful only in being spread.

Women and wine, game and deceit, make the wealth small, and the wants great. Benjamin Franklin

Great estates may venture more, but little boats should keep near shore. Benjamin Franklin

Sell not virtue to purchase wealth, nor liberty to purchase power. Benjamin Franklin

Many a man would have been worse, if his estate had been better. Benjamin Franklin

If you have no money in your pot, have some in your mouth. Benjamin Franklin

Get what you can, and what you get hold; tis the stone that will turn all your lead into gold. Benjamin Franklin

GENERAL

He who requires much from himself and little from others, will keep himself from being the object of resentment. Confucius

The great disgrace in the human race is the lack of pace to finish the race. John Taylor Wood

Shape up or ship out. US Navy

What actions are most excellent? To gladden the heart of a human being, to feed the hungry, to help the afflicted, to lighten the sorrow of the sorrowful, and to remove the wrongs of the injured.

Conquer a stingy person by generosity, a liar by truth, a cruel man by patience, and a bad man by goodness.

No fire like passion; no spark like hatred; no snare like folly; and no tyrant like greed.

Injustice anywhere is a threat to justice everywhere. Martin Luther King Jr.

Inscribed on the people's sword: Forgive him who wrongs you; join him who cuts you off; do good to him who does evil to you; and speak the truth even if it be against you.

The three best things: to be humble amidst the vissisitudes of fortune; to pardon when powerful; and to be generous with no strings attached.

MINDFULNESS

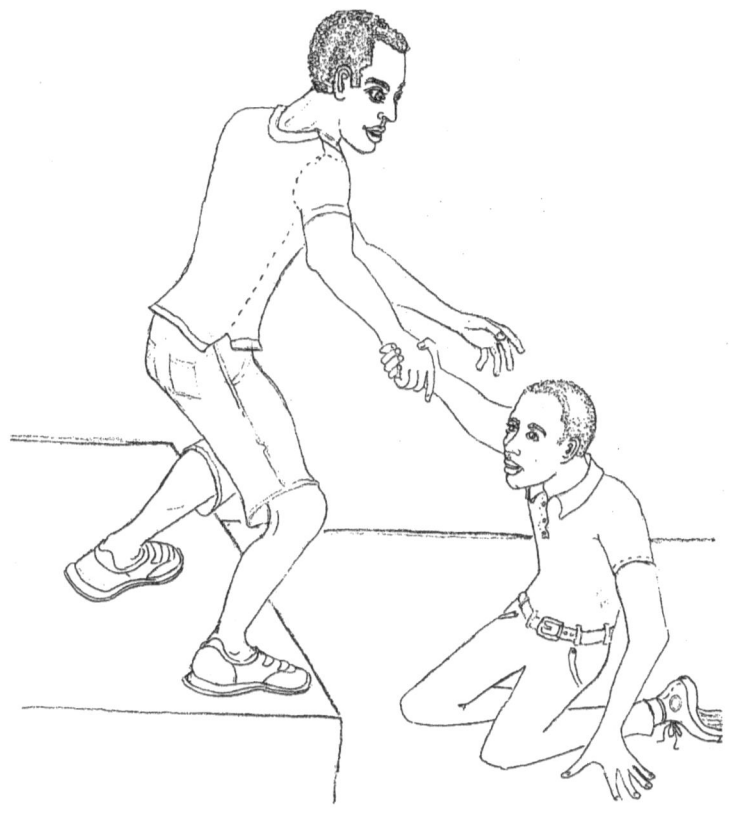

A good exercise for the heart is to bend down and help another up.

MINDFULNESS

ALONE

When the wolf is alone, he is a lion.

APPRECIATION

Don't cry because it is over. Smile because it happened.

CONSCIENCE

Are there tears? There is conscience.

He who cannot sleep finds his bed poorly made.

In matter of conscience, the law of the majority has no place.
Mahatma Gandhi

CONTENTMENT

Food supports life, contentment the soul.

Content is the philosopher's stone that turns all it touches into gold.
Benjamin Franklin

He that's content, have enough; he that complains, has too much.
Benjamin Franklin

END

Everything is always okay in the end, if it's not, then it is not the end.

FUTURE

Study the past if you would divine the future. Confucius

The best thing about the future is that it comes one day at a time.
Abraham Lincoln

Tis easy to see, hard to foresee. Benjamin Franklin

It may be fire, tomorrow it will be ashes.

GRIEF

The grief of tomorrow is not to be eaten today.

HEART

Tanks can be filled up, but a man's heart can never be closed.

If the heart be impure; all actions will be wrong.

The man grows old, not so his heart.

A good exercise for the heart is to bend down and help another up.

Two things that are bad for the heart … running up stairs and running down people.

IMAGINATION

Imagination is the highest kite one can fly.

Imagination is more important than knowledge.

MIND

The eyes are of little use if the mind be blind.

A head without a mind is a mere statue.

Man's mind once stretched by a new idea, never regains its original dimensions.

Laws and institutions must go hand in hand with the progress of the human mind. Thomas Jefferson

MISTAKE

A man who has committed a mistake and doesn't correct it, is committing another mistake. Confucius

When you find you have made a mess, clean it up before you rest. John Taylor Wood

To be wrong is nothing unless you continue to remember it.
Confucius

OLD

We do not cease to play because we are old, but we become old because we cease to play. Rufus Vernier

An old tree has a firm core.

When your friends begin to flatter you on how well you look, it's a sure sign you're getting old. Mark Twain

The gravity of old age is fairer than the flower of youth.

A clever woman is not old, though aged, but has the sweet sap of wit in her.

The older I get, the faster I was.

To survive old age, you can't be a wimp.

PRESENT

We mount the ladder step by step.

You have to believe every single day in a way you believe will make you feel good about your life … so that if it were over tomorrow, you'd be content with yourself.

We always make advance, say the tortoise i.e. Slow but sure.

Yesterday was history. Tomorrow is a mystery. Today is a gift. That's why it is called "the present."

Do it now!

Today is yesterday's pupil. Benjamin Franklin

It's not only later than you think – It's sooner then you suspect.

Never leave that till tomorrow which you can do today. Benjamin Franklin

REPENTANCE

Forethought is easy, repentance hard.

REPUTATION

Glass, china and reputation are easily cracked, and never well mended. Benjamin Franklin

SENSE

Good sense is a thing all need, few have, and none think they want. Benjamin Franklin

Some are weatherwise, some are otherwise. Benjamin Franklin

SHAME

Man is the only animal that blushes or needs to. Mark Twain

TIME

You may delay, but time will not. Benjamin Franklin

Backward, turn backward, oh time in your flight, make me a child again, just for tonight.

Time heals all wounds.

Do not squander time, for that's what life is made of. Benjamin Franklin

A stitch in time saves nine.

If you have time, don't wait for time. Benjamin Franklin

The waves flowing away chase those that preceed; in the world the new-born chase away the old, and they also pass away; no feast lasts forever.

Lost time is never seen again. Benjamin Franklin

Time is stronger than all things.

Time wounds all heels. Groucho Marx

YOUNG

The tree which is young you could have nipped off with your nail. You cannot afterward cut with an axe.

GENERAL

We can not lead someone else to the light when we are standing in the dark.

The study of existence prevents nonexistence. James Clifton

We do not see things the way they are. We see things as we are.

When you meet someone better than yourself, turn your thoughts to becoming his equal.

CONCENTRATION

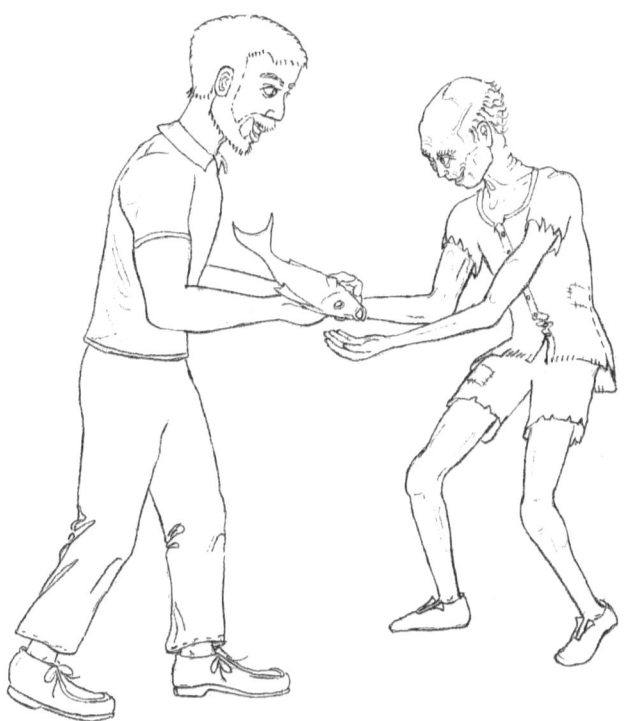

Give a man a fish and he can eat for a day; teach a man to fish and he can eat for a lifetime.

CONCENTRATION

CHARM

As charms are nonsense, nonsense is a charm. Benjamin Franklin

EMOTION

A boat which is swamped at sea may be bailed out, but a shipwreck of the affections is final.

FAILURE

Our greatest glory is never in falling, but in rising every time we fail.

Failure is success if we learn from it.

If your life is free of failures, than you're not taking enough risks.

FAULTS

Happy is the person who finds fault with himself instead of finding fault with others.

When you have faults, do not fear to abandon them. Confucius

You can bear your own faults, and why not a fault in your wife? Benjamin Franklin

Neglect mending a small fault, and 'twill soon be a great one. Benjamin Franklin

Love your enemies, for they will tell you your faults. Benjamin Franklin

Faults are thick when love is thin.

It is only with the eyes of others we see our own faults.

There are two kinds of folly, the one madness and the other ignorant. Plato

They know their own defects who search for defects of others.

Tis great confidence in a friend to tell him your faults, greater to tell him his. Benjamin Franklin

None but the well bred man knows how to confess a fault, or acknowledge himself in error. Benjamin Franklin

FOCUS

Reach high for stars that lie hidden in your soul. Dream deep, for every dream proceeds a goal.

Quit the bitchin and start the fixin. John Taylor Wood

Consider the postage stamp; its usefulness consists of the ability to stick to one thing till it gets there.

GOVERN (self)

He who can govern himself is fit to govern the world.

IDEALS

Keep your ideals high enough to inspire you and low enough to encourage you.

MODERATION

Eight different things to enjoy not in abundance, but in moderation: good labor, sleep, riches, journeying, love, warm water, bleeding and wine.

Joy and grief must be regulated by moderation.

Excess is to be avoided in all things.

The most intelligent people are those doing without, because they love what God loves and dislike the world God dislikes. Mohammad

NOISE

The noisy cat catches nothing.

PASSION

Do not come near one in a passion.

Were there no passions no one would build a house, marry, bring up children, or drive a trade.

PERSPECTIVE

If your only tool is a hammer, you tend to see every problem as a nail.

PATIENCE

Patience is the key to joy.

PLANNING

The 6 Ps: Prior Planning Prevents Piss Poor Performance.

Measure your cloth ten times; you can cut but once.

Lack of planning on your part doesn't constitute an emergency on my part.

Plans fail for lack of counsel, but with many advisors they succeed.

To gain a cat but lose a cow.

Don't descend into a well with a rotten rope.

SACRIFICE

For the nourishment of a day he sacrificed the food for a year.

SELF-DISCIPLNE

To abstain from desires is riches.

SIGHT

By closing the eyes, it has become dark.

You cannot drive a straight furrow without a straight eye.

What we see is what we get – except in pre-packaged strawberries.

TEACH

A teacher who is attempting to teach without inspiring the pupil to learn is hammering on cold iron. Horace Mann

God, parents and instructors can never be repaid. Benjamin Franklin

There are two ways of spreading light; to be the candle or the mirror that reflects it.

Give a man a fish and he can eat for a day; teach a man to fish and he can eat for a lifetime

THINKING

Nothing is good or bad, but thinking makes it so.

Our thoughts determine our responses to life. We are not victims of the world. To the extent that we control our thoughts, we control the world.

WEAKNESS

There are two kinds of weakness, that which breaks and that which bends.

WORRY

A day of worry is more exhausting than a week of work.

When I look back on all these worries I remember the old man who said on his deathbed that he had had a lot trouble in his life, most of which had never happened. Winston Churchill

GENERAL

Man thinks, God guides.

Don't let what you can not do interfere with what you can do.

Use it or lose it.

PURPOSE

God, grant me the serenity to accept the things I cannot change...

PURPOSE

ACCOMPLISHMENT

There are four steps to accomplishment: Plan purposefully. Prepare prayerfully. Proceed positively. Pursue persistently.

CAUSE

If you don't stand for something, you'll fall for anything.

CHANGE

It is only the wisest and the stupidest that cannot change. Confucius

CHALLENGE

The ultimate measure of a man is not where he stands in moments of comfort and convenience, but where he stands at times of challenge and controversy. Martin Luther King Jr.

God grant me the serenity to accept the things I cannot change; the courage to change the things I can; and the wisdom to know the difference.

COURAGE

To see what is right, and not do it, is want of courage, or principle. Confucius

Courage is resistance to fear, mastery of fear, not absence of fear.

Courage would fight, but discretion won't let him. Benjamin Franklin

CRITICAL

Let the refining and improving of your own life keep you so busy that you have little time to criticize others.

DEATH

We die as we live.

Death takes no bribes. Benjamin Franklin

Like opium production, the world manufacture of armament needs to be restricted. The sword is probably responsible for more misery in the world than opium. Mahatma Gandhi

DISPOSITION

A loving disposition is a river without a ripple.

DREAM

Reach high for stars lie hidden in your soul. Dream deep, for every dream proceeds a goal.

Nothing is impossible to the man who doesn't have to do it.

FAITH

I have therefore found it necessary to deny knowledge in order to make room for faith. Immanuel Kant

FAMILY

Tis a strange forest that has no rotten wood in it; and a strange kindred that all are good in it. Benjamin Franklin

A true sign of a good man is if he loves his father and mother. Gurdjieff

FRIENDSHIP

There are three faithful friends, an old wife, an old dog, and ready money. Benjamin Franklin

He who has no fire in himself cannot warm others.

Without a clear mirror a women cannot see her face; without a true friend a man cannot discern the nature of his actions.

Begin the day with friendliness, and only friends you'll find. Yes, greet the dawn with happiness; keep happy thoughts in mind.

A friend is someone who reaches for your hand and touches your heart.

Be civil to all; sociable to many; familiar with few; friend to one; enemy to none.

The art of acceptance is the art of making someone who has done you a small favor wish that they might have done you a greater one.

A father's a treasure; a brother's a comfort; a friend is both. Benjamin Franklin

He who seeks a friend without a fault remains without one.

A single coal does not burn well; a companionless traveler finds the journey tedious.

A man without a friend is a left hand without the right.

A friend at hand is better than relations at a distance.

Have no friends not equal to yourself. Confucius

GOD

There are four things God cannot do: He cannot lie; He cannot die; He cannot deny himself; and He cannot look favorably on sin.

God has no religion. Mahatma Gandhi

The noblest work of God? Man? Who found it out? Man. Mark Twain

GOOD

The more a good tree grows, the more shade it affords.

When someone does something good, applaud! You will make two people happy.

There is so much good in the worst of us and so much bad in the rest of us that it behooves all of us not to talk about the rest of us.

The good is beautiful. Plato

HAPPINESS

Most people are as happy as they make up their minds to be.

Happiness is an inside job.

Happiness is not being pained in body or troubled in mind. Thomas Jefferson

Happiness is not an ideal of reason but of imagination. Immanuel Kant

Good friends, good books and a sleepy conscience: this is the ideal life. Mark Twain

Happiness is not an absence of problems; but the ability to deal with them.

How many things are there which I do not want? Socrates

The main thing needed to make men happy is intelligence. Bertrand Russell

The gift of happiness belongs to those who unwrap it.

Happiness held is the seed; happiness shared is the flower.

Don't be sad. Don't be mad. Don't be bad. Just be glad. John Taylor Wood

Happiness is a voyage, not a destination.

Happiness is like crystal. When it shines the most, it soon shows cracks.

HOPE

He that lives upon hope will die fasting. Benjamin Franklin

Hope is a waking dream. Aristotle

JUSTICE

Aggressiveness unopposed becomes a dangerous disease. Jimmy Carter

Only he can be just who is able to put himself in the position of others. Gurdjieff

Injustice anywhere is a threat to justice everywhere. Martin Luther King Jr.

LAUGHTER

Laughter is the best medicine.

LAW

All persons ought to endeavor to follow what is right, and not what is established. Aristotle

Man, when perfected, is the best of animals, but, when separated from the law and justice, he is the worst of all. Aristotle

The only stable state is the one in which all men are equal before the law. Aristotle

LIFE

A long life may not be good enough, but a good life is long enough. Benjamin Franklin

Variety is the spice of life.

The man who views the world at 50 the same as he did at 20 has wasted 30 years of his life. Muhammad Ali

He that lives with dogs, shall rise up with fleas. Benjamin Franklin

Wish not too much to live long as to live well. Benjamin Franklin

When you can do the common things of life in an uncommon way, you'll command the attention of the world. George Washington Carver

When we remember that we are all mad, the mysteries disappear and life stands explained. Mark Twain

Live and learn, and a great life you'll earn. John Taylor Wood

Life like a fire begins in smoke, ends in ashes.

Life with fools consists in drinking; with wise men, living's thinking. Benjamin Franklin

Life is a grindstone, whether it grinds you down or polishes you up depends on what you're made of. Jacob Braude

Illegetimi Non Carborundum. (Latin- Don't let the bastards (illegitimate) grind you down.)

Life can only be understood backwards, but it must be lived forwards.

It's a funny thing about life; if you refuse to accept anything but the best, you often get it.

Life is the first gift, love is the second, and understanding is the third.

Everything done in your entire life should be directed towards making you a better person.

Live each day as if there is no tomorrow.

Have in life the force of a lion, the sagacity of an elephant, and the sweetness of a lamb.

Here is a test to see if your mission on earth is complete: If you're alive, it isn't. Richard Bach

We make a living by what we get, but we make a life by what we give.

When are you done? When you're not having fun. John Taylor Wood

LOVE

The ultimate lesson all of us have to learn is unconditional love, which includes not only others but ourselves as well.

To love a thing makes the eye blind, the ear deaf.

Faults are thick where love is thin.

You will not enter paradise until you believe, and you will not believe until you love one another.

What is most excellent in a human being? A friendly disposition. Mohammad

He is not of us who is not affectionate to the little ones and does not respect the reputation of the old.

To love a thing means wanting it to live. Confucius

MANKIND

The superior man is satisfied and composed; the mean man is always full of distress. Confucius

If a man hasn't found something that he will die for, he isn't fit to live. Martin Luther King Jr.

Not in time, place or circumstance, but in man lies success.

Among men some are jewels and some are pebbles.

Man is a tool-making animal. Benjamin Franklin

Treat humanity as an end and not as a means to reach an end. Emmanuel Kant

Reading makes a full man, meditation a profound man, disclosure a clear man. Benjamin Franklin

Man without sense is like a blind man with a looking glass.

MARRIAGE

A man without a wife, is but half a man. Benjamin Franklin

Marry above thy match, and thou'lt get a master.

Keep your eyes wide open before marriage, half shut afterwards.
Benjamin Franklin

MISERY

Pain and suffering are inevitable, but misery is an option.

MOTHERS

Poor mothers: there is one thing sadder than to see their children die
– to see them lead evil lives. Victor Hugo

My son's my son until he gets a wife, but my daughters my daughter
all of her life.

NECESSITY

Necessity never made a good bargain. Benjamin Franklin

Necessity is the mother of invention.

NONVIOLENCE

Nonviolence is a powerful and just weapon unique in history, which
cuts without wounding and enables the man who wields it. It is a
sword that heals. Martin Luther King Jr.

Nonviolence is not a garment to be put on and off at will, its seat
is in the heart and it must be an inseparable part of our very being.
Mahatma Gandhi

OPPORTUNITY

If you are looking for a big opportunity, seek out a big problem.

A wise man will make more opportunities than he finds.

In the middle of difficulty lies opportunity.

An optimist sees an opportunity in every calamity; a pessimist sees a calamity in every opportunity.

One door is shut, but a thousand are open.

PARENTS

Parents say, "Our boy is growing up." They forget his life is shortening.

We never wander so far away as when we think we know the way.

PRAYING

Prayer is not asking. – It is a longing of the soul. Mahatma Gandhi

Serving God is doing good to man, but praying is thought an easier service, and therefore more generally chosen. Benjamin Franklin

PROBLEM

To any problem, you can choose to ignore or to cure. John Taylor Wood

The best way to solve any problem is to remove its cause. Martin Luther King Jr.

RELIGION

A man knowing law, but without God's fear, is a man having the key of the inner door, but not of the outer chamber.

How could they say that my religion was a "race hate" religion (Islam)? After all the plunder and enslavement and domination of my people by white Christians was in the name of white supremacy. Muhammad Ali

My karma ran over my dogma.

A man devoid of religion is like a horse without a bridle.

I consider myself a Hindu, Christian, Moslem, Jew, Buddhist, and Confucian. Mahatma Gandhi

Respect every religion. Gurdjieff

All religions must be tolerated … For … every man must get to heaven his own way. Frederick The Great

Science without religion is lame, Religion without science is blind. Albert Einstein

Many have quarreled about religion, that never practiced it. Benjamin Franklin

SERVITUDE

The best of God's servants are those who when seen remind you of God; and the worse of God's servants are those who spread tales to do mischief and separate friends, and look for the faults of the good.

The most important single ingredient in the formula of success is knowing how to get along with people. Theodore Roosevelt

The best people are those who are useful to others.

STANDARD

Hold yourself responsible for a higher standard than anyone else expects of you.

SMILE

Most smiles start with another smile.

SORROW

Sorrow is to the soul what a worm is to wood.

TOOL

The dinner ended, we value no more the spoon.

No one can sew without a needle; no one can row a boat without water.

There was never a good knife made of bad steel. Benjamin Franklin

TRUTH

By digging and digging the truth is discovered.

A lie stands on one leg, truth on two. Benjamin Franklin

Truth is the most valuable thing we have. Let us economize it. Confucius

It is man that makes truth great, not truth that makes man great. Confucious

VALUES

It's not hard to make decisions when you know what your values are.

WAR

As in law as in war, the longest purse finaly wins. Immanuel Kant

We make war that we may live in peace. Aristotle

YOURSELF

The best fighting is against yourself.

UNDERSTANDING

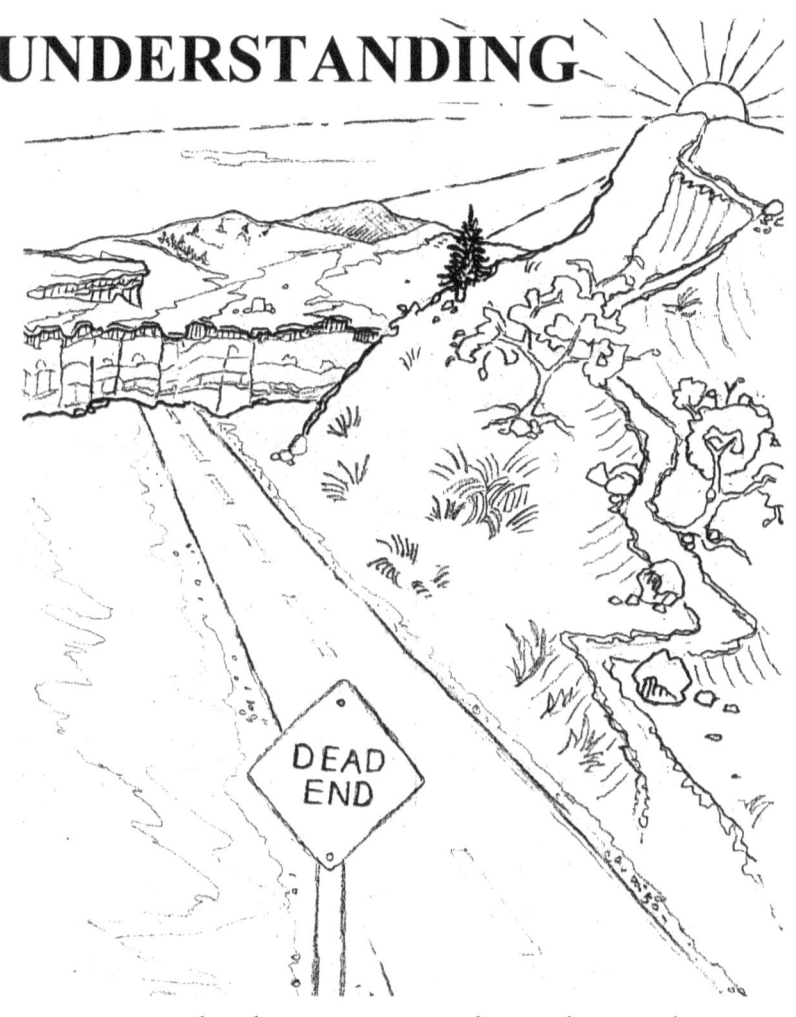

Do not think you are on the right road
because it is a well-beaten path.

UNDERSTANDING

APPEARANCE

You can't tell a book or a person by its cover.

BEAUTY

The beautiful is that which pleases universally without a concept.
Immanuel Kant

Beauty is in the eye of the beholder.

Everything has beauty, but not everyone sees it. Confucius

COMPROMISE

Better bend than break.

COOPERATION

With one hand I do not even tie a knot.

You can not clap with one hand alone.

God gives food, but does he cook it and put it in the mouth?

DOUBT

To believe is very dull. To doubt is intensely engrossing. Oscar Wilde

Doubt destroys faith as salt does honey.

EDUCATION

Education is what survives when what has been learned has been
forgotten. B.F. Skinner

The roots of education are bitter, but the fruit is sweet. Aristotle

Genius without education is like silver in the mine. Benjamin
Franklin

Education is the best provision for old age. Aristotle

EGO

Can the boat bear the ship's mast?

ENEMY

The people may be made to follow a course of action, but they may not be made to understand it. Confucius

The physician who cured the stripped tiger of his sickness became his prey.

It takes your enemy and your friend, working together, to hurt you to the heart; one to slander you and the other to get the news to you. Confucius

EVIL

No evil can happen to a good man, either in life or after death. Socrates

No rest for the wicked.

No restraint in wickedness for those not fearing God.

The mice will play while the cat is away.

Keeping away from the mire is better than washing it off.

EXPERIENCE

Experience teaches a dear school, and fools can learn in no other, and scarcely in that. Benjamin Franklin

FEAR

The only thing we have to fear is fear itself. Franklin Delano Roosevelt

FREEDOM

It is the goodness of God that in our country we have those three unspeakable things: freedom of speech, freedom of conscience, and the prudence never to practice either of them. Mark Twain

A free society is one where it is safe to be unpopular. Adlai Stevenson

HUMANITY

Treat humanity as an end and not as a means to reach an end. Immanuel Kant

IDLENESS

An idle brain is the devil's workshop.

Only help him who is not idle. Gurdjieff

INSIGHT

Ah, the insight of hindsight.

INTELLIGENCE

The most intelligent people are the people doing without because they love what God loves and dislikes. Mohammad

Experience is the looking-glass of intellect.

Two heads are better than one.

Your brain becomes a mind when it becomes fortified with knowledge.

Do not think you are on the right road because it is a well-beaten path.

KNOWLEDGE

I have therefore found it necessary to deny knowledge in order to make room for faith. Immanuel Kant

Real knowledge is to know the extent of one's ignorance. Confucius

He who leaves home in search of knowledge walks in the path of God. Mohammed

He without knowledge is blind.

Knowledge overcomes ignorance as sunlight does darkness.

There are three things extremely hard: steel, a diamond and to know one's self. Benjamin Franklin

Knowledge is our friend in the desert, our society of solitude, our companion when lack of friends; it guides us to happiness, it sustains us in misery, it serves as an armor against enemies. Mohammad

LEARNING

One void of learning is a beast.

Being ignorant is not so shameful as being unwilling to learn.

It is possible to learn things from an enemy we can't learn from a friend.

Learn from the skillful: He that teaches himself, hath a fool for his master. Benjamin Franklin

Love to learn, so you learn to live. John Taylor Wood

Tim was so learned, that he could name a horse in nine languages. So ignorant, that he bought a cow to ride on. Benjamin Franklin

I am always ready to learn although I do not always like being taught. Winston Churchill

Plants of learning must be watered with the rain of tears.

The learned fool writes his nonsense in better language than the unlearned, but still tis nonsense. Benjamin Franklin

Being ignorant is not so much a shame, as being unwilling to learn. Benjamin Franklin

Wise men learn by others harms; fools by their own. Benjamin Franklin

Most of the learning in use, is of no great use. Benjamin Franklin

If thou has wit and learning, add to it wisdom and modesty. Benjamin Franklin

Learning without thought is labor lost, thought without learning is perilous. Confucius

LIBERTY

Order without liberty and liberty without order are equally destructive. Theodore Roosevelt

The shepherd drives the wolf from the sheep's throat, for which the sheep thanks the shepherd as his liberator, while the wolf denounces him for the same act as the destroyer of liberty. Abraham Lincoln

Liberty consists in the power of doing that which is permitted by law. Cicero

The tree of liberty must be refreshed from time to time with the blood of patriots and tyrants. Thomas Jefferson

LISTEN

If you want to be listened to, you should put in time listening.

NEGATIVE

Every rose has a thorn.

PERSON

It takes a good person to know a good person; unfortunately few know me. John Taylor Wood

POTENTIAL

Pearls unpolished shine not.

SCIENCE

Today's adventures in science will create tomorrow's America. Gilbert Co. motto

Science without religion is materialism. Religion without science is superstition.

VARIETY

Variety is the spice of life.

VIRTUE

Plato's four cardinal virtues: wisdom, courage, temperature, justice.

Virtue may not always make a face handsome, but vice will certainly make it ugly. Benjamin Franklin

Much virtue in herbs, little in men. Benjamin Franklin

Search others for their virtues, thy self for thy vices. Benjamin Franklin

Fine words and an insinuating appearance are seldom associated with true virtue. Confucius

To be able to practice five things everywhere under heaven constitutes perfect virtue … gratuity, generosity of soul, sincerity, earnestness and kindness. Confucius

WISDOM

If a man goes not after wisdom, it does not come to him.

Wisdom is the gray hair unto men.

The wise know how to quit the world before the world quits them.

The wise man draws more advantage from his enemies than the fool from his friends. Benjamin Franklin

The doors of wisdom are never shut. Benjamin Franklin

Riches diminish in the using, wisdom increases by use.

GENERAL

You can't keep a good person down.

Have in life the force of a lion, the sagacity of the elephant, and the sweetness of a lamb.

Always prefer to believe the best of everybody ... It saves so much trouble.

A person can be evaluated by their parental upbringing, education, health, religion they practice and the company they keep. John Taylor Wood

The people may be made to follow a course of action, but they may not be made to understand it. Confucius

Two heads are better than one.

He that best understands the world, least likes it. Benjamin Franklin

SPEECH

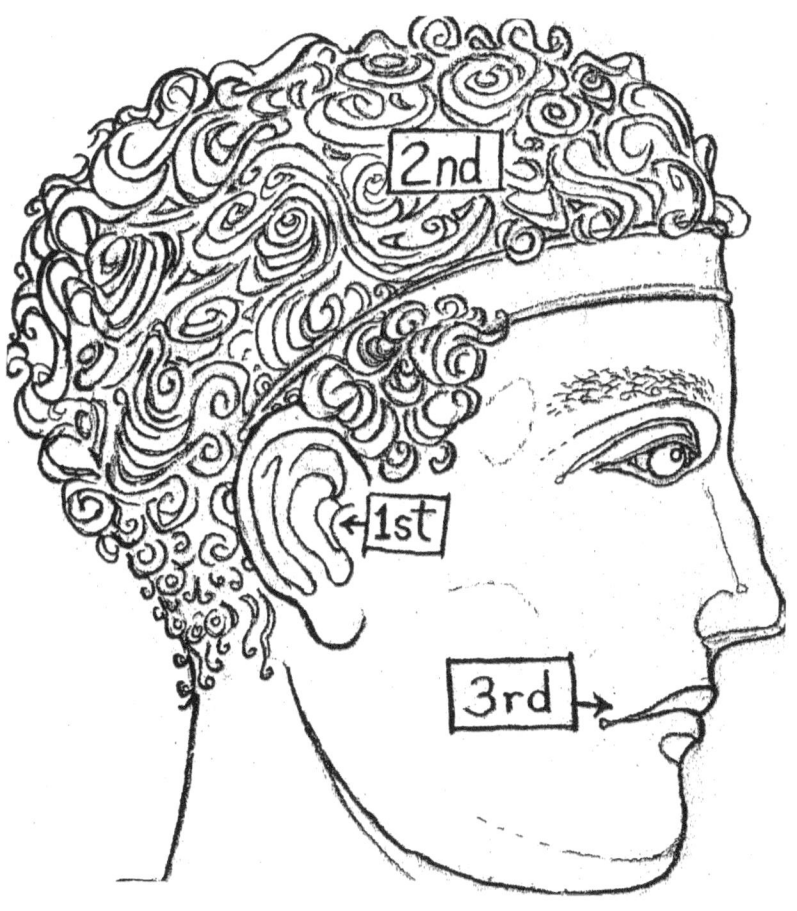

SPEECH

CONVERSATION

A man's conversation is a mirror of his heart.

The real art of conversation is not only to say the right thing in the right place but to leave unsaid the wrong thing at the tempting moment. Dorothy MacDonald

COUNSELED

He that won't be counseled, can't be helped. Benjamin Franklin

DANCE

Hence it is from the representation of things spoken by means of posture and gesture that the whole art of dance has been elaborated. Plato

GRATITUDE

Whoever does not express his gratitude to people will never be grateful to God. Mohammad

MOUTH

Engage brain before mouth.

Loose lips can sink big ships. US Navy

The heart of a fool is in his mouth, but the mouth of a wise man is in his heart. Benjamin Franklin

When you speak to man, look on his eyes; when he speaks to thee' look at his mouth. Benjamin Franklin

MUSIC

Music has the power of producing a certain effect on the moral character of the soul, and if it has the power to do this, it is clear that the youth must be directed to music and must be educated in it. Aris

Music produces a kind of pleasure which human nature cannot do without. Confucious

Because more than anything else rhythm and harmony find their way to the inmost soul and take strongest hold upon it, bringing with them and imparting grace, if one is rightfully trained. Plato

Without music life would be a mistake. Friedrich Nietzche

After science, that which comes nearest to expressing the inexpressible is music. Aldous Huxley

Wagner's music is better than it sounds. Mark Twain

ORATORY

My father gave me these hints on speech-making. "Be sincere ... Be brief ... Be seated." James Roosevelt

Nothing is so unbelievable that oratory cannot make it acceptable. Cicero

Trying to settle a problem with oratory is like attempting to unsnarl a traffic jam by blowing horns.

Liberty doesn't work as well in practice as it does in speeches. Will Rogers

There is no power like oratory. Caesar controlled men by exciting fears, Cicero by their passions. The influence of one perished, that of the other continues to this day. Henry Clay

PRONOUNCE

Everybody has the right to pronounce foreign names as he chooses. Winston Churchill

SILENCE

As we must account for every idle word, so we must for every idle silence. Benjamin Franklin

SPEAK

Speak softly and carry a big stick. Theodore Roosevelt

I disapprove of what you say, but I will defend to the death your right to say it. Voltaire

He that speaks much is much mistaken. Benjamin Franklin

He that would live in peace and ease, must not speak all he knows, nor judge all he sees. Benjamin Franklin

Consider what people think of you – not what they say. Gurdjieff

Whoever believes in one God and the Hereafter, let him speak what is good or remain silent. Mohammad

Courage is what it takes to stand up and speak; courage is also what it takes to sit down and listen.

Never let a day go by without giving at least three people a compliment.

You should speak ill of no man, and speak all the good you know of everybody.

Two ears to one tongue; therefore hear twice as much as you speak.

Hear no ill of a friend, nor speak any of an enemy. Benjamin Franklin

A great river makes no noise.

When one has learned to speak prudently, why should we think of his youth or age? May not a lamp burn bright though held in the hand of an infant?

Surrender is purity of speech and hospitality. Mohammad

TONGUE

A slip of the foot you may soon recover, but a slip of the tongue you may never recover. Benjamin Franklin

Tongue double, brings trouble. Benjamin Franklin

Since I can not govern my own tongue, tho' within my own teeth, how can I hope to govern the tongues of others? Benjamin Franklin

To slip on the pavement is better than to slip with the tongue.

The heart is the treasury of the tongue.

A perfect Muslim is one from whose tongue and hands mankind is safe. Mohammad

Man's tongue is soft, and bone doth lack, yet a stroke there with may break a man's back. Benjamin Franklin

WIT

There are no fools so troublesome as those that have wit. Benjamin Franklin

WORDS

A picture is worth a 1000 words, but 1000 words can be written faster than a picture can be made. John Taylor Wood

Here comes the orator! With his flood of words, and drop of reason. Benjamin Franklin

A famine may cease, but abusive words will be always remembered.

Kind words can be short and easy to speak, but their echoes are truly endless.

John Taylor Wood

Man does not live by words alone, despite the fact that sometimes he has to eat them. Adlai Stevenson

VOCATION

Man is the slave of money.

VOCATION

CLERGY/SCHOLAR/TEACHER

The ink of the scholar is more sacred than the blood of the martyr. Mohammad

Every religion has a distinctive virtue and the distinctive virtue of Surrender is modesty.

The pious need no memorial; their deeds are their memorial.

When a culture feels that its end has come, it sends for a priest. Karl Kraus

How strange a thing this is! The priest telleth me that the soul is worth all the gold in the world, and the merchants say it is not worth a clipped piece of silver. Oscar Wilde

Man is great only when he is kneeling. Pope Pius XII

Not our logical faculty, but our imaginative one is king over us. I might say, priest and prophet to lead us to heaven-ward, magician and wizard to lead us hell-ward. Thomas Carlyle

Good character is half the faith.

The search for truth is not a trade by which a man can support himself. For a priest it is a supreme peril. Alfred Loisy

ADMINISTRATOR/MILITARY

The radical invents the views. When he has worn them out, the conservative adopts them. Mark Twain

A good leader takes a little more than their share of the blame, and a little less than their share of the credit.

You may give a man an office, but you cannot give him discretion. Benjamin Franklin

Industry pays debts, despair increases them. Benjamin Franklin

The business of government is to keep government out of business – that is, unless business needs government aid. Will Rogers

Human salvation lies in the hands of the creatively maladjusted. Martin Luther King Jr.

Only one man in a thousand is a leader of men. The other 999 follow women. Mark Twain

Leadership is the power to evoke the right response in other people.

Good order is the foundation of all good things.

Those who make peaceful revolution impossible will make violent revolution inevitable. John F. Kennedy

In a country well governed poverty is something to be ashamed of. In a country badly governed wealth is something to be ashamed of. Confucius

The price of greatness is responsibility. Winston Churchill

It is with law as with dykes. - In whatever part they are broken, the rest will become useless. No ease for the mouth when one tooth is broken.

Corruption begins from the head, i.e. from the chiefs.

The old law of an eye for an eye leaves everybody blind. Mahatma Gandhi

A country that is governed by even its national army can never be morally free. Mahatma Gandhi

Shape up or ship out. US Navy

MERCHANT/FARMER/ENTERTAINER

When friend deals with a friend let the bargain be clear and well penn'd that they may continue friends to the end. Benjamin Franklin

Regardless of the company you are working for, never forget the most important product you're selling is yourself.

Some see private enterprise as a predatory target to be shot, others as a cow to be milked, but few are those who see it as a sturdy horse pulling a wagon. Winston Churchill

I am only a public entertainer who understands his time. Pablo Picasso

When you dance with your customer, let him lead.

There is more credit and satisfaction in being a first-rate truck driver than a tenth-rate executive. B.C. Forbes

Beware of the young doctor and old barber. Benjamin Franklin

A heart free from care is better than a full purse.

Capital as such is not evil, it is wrong use that is evil. Capital in some form or other will always be needed. Mahatma Gandhi

Being an entertainer especially in times like these, is a real public service. Linda Ronstadt

American business needs a lifting purpose greater than the struggles of materialism. Herbert Hoover

If you were to sell your character, would you get full retail, or would it go for a bargain-basement price?

A plowman on his legs is higher than a gentleman on his knees. Benjamin Franklin

In this world nothing can be certain but death and taxes. Benjamin Franklin

Money-getters are the benefactors of our race. To them … are we indebted for our institutions of learning, and of art, our academies, colleges and churches. P.T. Barnum

Getting something for free is worth what you pay for it.

Capitalism with greed control is compelling. John Taylor Wood

We work to become, not to acquire. Elbert Hubbard

Work expands so as to fill the time available for its completion. Northcote Parkinson

There are two times in a man's life when he should not speculate: when he can't afford it, when he can. Mark Twain

LABORER/PUBLIC SERVANT

A wise man will desire no more than what he may get justly, use soberly, distribute cheerfully, and leave contently. Benjamin Franklin

He that sows thorns, should never go barefoot. Benjamin Franklin

A callous on the hand is as noble as a degree on the wall.

At the working man's house hunger looks in but dares not enter. Benjamin Franklin

If you don't want to work, you have to work to earn enough money so that you won't have to work. Ogden Nash

Pound to fit. Paint to finish. J.I. Case

Keep your nose to the grindstone.

GENERAL

Choose a job you love, and you will never have to work a day in your life. Confucius

God gives all things to industry. Benjamin Franklin

Poverty is the parent of revolution and crime. Aristotle

Man is the slave of money.

Work well done is art.

While you both are working you live in a house. When you retire, it is a home.

All paid jobs absorb and degrade the mind. Aristotle

Time is money. Benjamin Franklin

In this world nothing can be certain but death and taxes. Benjamin Franklin

In competition one person's success is another's failure. John Taylor Wood

Pleasure in the job put perfection in the work. Aristotle

ORDER YOUR FAVORITE QUOTE

Philosophize Inc. can have your favorite quote preserved in an artistic manner. Display your cherished quote to remind you and others of a guide to a good life.

We can engrave, carve, print, burn or emboss words on wood, metal, glass, stone, paper, plastic, leather or cloth.

Correspond with us at: www.philosophizeinc.com

Detail your requirement, and we will quote your price and delivery.

Our products will get a small logo ɹTw.

Enjoy these words of wisdom from the masters of our planet. Their guidance from God leads to spreading the good way to live throughout the universe.

These quotes will guide you on your paths to Nirvana.

My Favorite Quotes:
John Taylor Wood
1/20/10

May you have....

Enough happiness to keep you sweet
    Enough trials to keep you strong

Enough sorrow to keep you human
    Enough hope to keep you happy

Enough failure to keep you humble
    Enough success to keep you eager

Enough friends to give you comfort
    Enough wealth to meet your needs

Enough enthusiasm to look forward
    Enough faith to banish depression

Enough determination to make each
    Day a better day than yesterday

If you can think- and not make thoughts your aim,
If you can meet with triumph and disaster
And treat those two imposters just the same;
If you can fill the unforgiving minute
With sixty seconds worth of distance run,
Yours is the earth and everything that's in it,
And-which is more- you'll be a man, my son!
    Rudyard Kipling

Act in such a rational way that what you do could become a universal law.

Immanuel Kant

Life is a grindstone. Whether it grinds you down or polishes you up depends on what you're made of.   Jacob Braude

Illegitmi non carborundum. (Don't let the bastards grind you down.)

Quit the bitchin and start the fixin. John Taylor Wood

Yesterday was history. Tomorrow is a mystery. Today is a gift. That's why it's called the PRESENT.

If you are going through hell, KEEP GOING. Winston Churchill

Aggressive fighting for the right is the noblest sport the world affords.

Theodore Roosevelt

INDEX BY SUBJECT

INDEX BY AUTHOR

www.ingramcontent.com/pod-product-compliance
Lightning Source LLC
Chambersburg PA
CBHW020336290526
45785CB00005B/2041